Told after Supper

by

Jerome Klapka Jerome

First published 2008

ISBN 978-1-4092-2944-5

Printed and bound by lulu.com

Table of Contents

INTRODUCTORY

It was Christmas Eve. I begin this way because it is the proper, orthodox, respectable way to begin, and I have been brought up in a proper, orthodox, respectable way, and taught to always do the proper, orthodox, respectable thing; and the habit clings to me.

Of course, as a mere matter of information it is quite unnecessary to mention the date at all. The experienced reader knows it was Christmas Eve, without my telling him. It always is Christmas Eve, in a ghost story.

Christmas Eve is the ghosts' great gala night. On Christmas Eve they hold their annual fete. On Christmas Eve everybody in Ghostland who *is* anybody—or rather, speaking of ghosts, one should say, I suppose, every nobody who *is* any nobody—comes out to show himself or herself, to see and to be seen, to promenade about and display their winding-sheets and grave-clothes to each other, to criticise one another's style, and sneer at one another's complexion.

"Christmas Eve parade", as I expect they themselves term it, is a function, doubtless, eagerly prepared for and looked forward to throughout Ghostland, especially the swagger set, such as the murdered Barons, the crime-stained Countesses, and the Earls who came over with the Conqueror, and assassinated their relatives, and died raving mad.

Hollow moans and fiendish grins are, one may be sure, energetically practised up. Blood-curdling shrieks and marrow-freezing gestures are probably rehearsed for weeks beforehand. Rusty chains and gory daggers are over-hauled, and put into good working order; and sheets and shrouds, laid carefully by from the previous year's show, are taken down and shaken out, and mended, and aired.

Oh, it is a stirring night in Ghostland, the night of December the twenty-fourth!

Ghosts never come out on Christmas night itself, you may have noticed. Christmas Eve, we suspect, has been too much for them; they are not used to excitement. For about a week after Christmas Eve, the gentlemen ghosts, no doubt, feel as if they were all head, and go about making solemn resolutions to themselves that they will stop in next Christmas Eve; while lady spectres are contradictory and snappish, and liable to burst into tears and leave the room hurriedly on being spoken to, for no perceptible cause whatever.

Ghosts with no position to maintain—mere middle-class ghosts—occasionally, I believe, do a little haunting on off-nights: on All-hallows Eve, and at Midsummer; and some will even run up for a mere local event—to celebrate, for instance, the anniversary of the hanging of somebody's grandfather, or to prophesy a misfortune.

He does love prophesying a misfortune, does the average British ghost. Send him out to prognosticate trouble to somebody, and he is happy. Let him force his way into a peaceful home, and turn the whole house upside down by foretelling a funeral, or predicting a bankruptcy, or hinting at a coming disgrace, or some other terrible disaster, about which nobody in their senses want to know sooner they could possibly help, and the prior knowledge of which can serve no useful purpose whatsoever, and he feels that he is combining duty with pleasure. He would never forgive himself if anybody in his family had a trouble and he had not been there for a couple of months beforehand, doing silly tricks on the lawn, or balancing himself on somebody's bed-rail.

Then there are, besides, the very young, or very conscientious ghosts with a lost will or an undiscovered number weighing heavy on their minds, who will haunt steadily all the year round; and also the fussy ghost, who is indignant at having been buried in the dust-bin or in the village pond, and who never gives the parish a single night's quiet until somebody has paid for a first-class funeral for him.

But these are the exceptions. As I have said, the average orthodox ghost does his one turn a year, on Christmas Eve, and is satisfied.

Why on Christmas Eve, of all nights in the year, I never could myself understand. It is invariably one of the most dismal of nights to be out in—cold, muddy, and wet. And besides, at Christmas time, everybody has quite enough to put up with in the way of a houseful of living relations, without wanting the ghosts of any dead ones mooning about the place, I am sure.

There must be something ghostly in the air of Christmas—something about the close, muggy atmosphere that draws up the ghosts, like the dampness of the summer rains brings out the frogs and snails.

And not only do the ghosts themselves always walk on Christmas Eve, but live people always sit and talk about them on Christmas Eve. Whenever five or six English-speaking people meet round a fire on Christmas Eve, they start telling each other ghost stories. Nothing satisfies us on Christmas Eve but to hear each other tell authentic anecdotes about spectres. It is a genial, festive season, and we love to muse upon graves, and dead bodies, and murders, and blood.

There is a good deal of similarity about our ghostly experiences; but this of course is not our fault but the fault ghosts, who never will try any new performances, but always will keep steadily to old, safe business. The consequence is that, when you have been at one Christmas Eve party, and heard six people relate their adventures with spirits, you do not require to hear any more ghost stories. To listen to any further ghost stories after that would be like sitting out two farcical comedies, or taking in two comic journals; the repetition would become wearisome.

There is always the young man who was, one year, spending the Christmas at a country house, and, on Christmas Eve, they put him to sleep in the west wing. Then in the middle of the night, the room door quietly opens and somebody—generally a lady in her night-dress—walks slowly in, and comes and sits on the bed. The young man thinks it must be one of the visitors, or some relative of the family, though he does not remember having previously seen her, who, unable to go to sleep, and feeling lonesome, all by herself, has come into his room for a chat. He has no idea it is a ghost: he is so unsuspicious. She does not speak, however; and, when he looks again, she is gone!

The young man relates the circumstance at the breakfast-table next morning, and asks each of the ladies present if it were she who was his visitor. But they all assure him that it was not, and the host, who has grown deadly pale, begs him to say no more about the matter, which strikes the young man as a singularly strange request.

After breakfast the host takes the young man into a corner, and explains to him that what he saw was the ghost of a lady who had been murdered in that very bed, or who had murdered somebody else there—it does not really matter which: you can be a ghost by murdering somebody else or by being murdered yourself, whichever you prefer. The murdered ghost is, perhaps, the more popular; but, on the other hand, you can frighten people better if you are the murdered one, because then you can show your wounds and do groans.

Then there is the sceptical guest—it is always 'the guest' who gets let in for this sort of thing, by-the-bye. A ghost never thinks much of his own family: it is 'the guest' he likes to haunt who after listening to the host's ghost story, on Christmas Eve, laughs at it, and says that he does not believe there are such things as ghosts at all; and that he will sleep in the haunted chamber that very night, if they will let him.

Everybody urges him not to be reckless, but he persists in his foolhardiness, and goes up to the Yellow Chamber (or whatever colour the haunted room may be) with a light heart and a candle, and wishes them all good-night, and shuts the door.

Next morning he has got snow-white hair.

He does not tell anybody what he has seen: it is too awful.

There is also the plucky guest, who sees a ghost, and knows it is a ghost, and watches it, as it comes into the room and disappears through the wainscot, after which, as the ghost does not seem to be coming back, and there is nothing, consequently, to be gained by stopping awake, he goes to sleep.

He does not mention having seen the ghost to anybody, for fear of frightening them—some people are so nervous about ghosts,—but determines to wait for the next night, and see if the apparition appears again.

It does appear again, and, this time, he gets out of bed, dresses himself and does his hair, and follows it; and then discovers a secret passage leading from the bedroom down into the beer-cellar,- -a passage which, no doubt, was not unfrequently made use of in the bad old days of yore.

After him comes the young man who woke up with a strange sensation in the middle of the night, and found his rich bachelor uncle standing by his bedside. The rich uncle smiled a weird sort of smile and vanished. The young man immediately got up and looked at his watch. It had stopped at half-past four, he having forgotten to wind it.

He made inquiries the next day, and found that, strangely enough, his rich uncle, whose only nephew he was, had married a widow with eleven children at exactly a quarter to twelve, only two days ago.

The young man does not attempt to explain the circumstance. All he does is to vouch for the truth of his narrative.

And, to mention another case, there is the gentleman who is returning home late at night, from a Freemasons' dinner, and who, noticing a light issuing from a ruined abbey, creeps up, and looks through the keyhole. He sees the ghost of a 'grey sister' kissing the ghost of a brown monk, and is so inexpressibly shocked and frightened that he faints on the spot, and is discovered there the next morning, lying in a heap against the door, still speechless, and with his faithful latch-key clasped tightly in his hand.

All these things happen on Christmas Eve, they are all told of on Christmas Eve. For ghost stories to be told on any other evening than the evening of the twenty-fourth of December would be impossible in English society as at present regulated. Therefore, in introducing the sad but authentic ghost stories that follow hereafter, I feel that it is unnecessary to inform the student of Anglo-Saxon literature that the date on which they were told and on which the incidents took place was—Christmas Eve.

Nevertheless, I do so.

NOW THE STORIES CAME TO BE TOLD

IT WAS CHRISTMAS EVE! Christmas Eve at my Uncle John's; Christmas Eve (There is too much 'Christmas Eve' about this book. I can see that myself. It is beginning to get monotonous even to me. But I don't see how to avoid it now) at No. 47 Laburnham Grove, Tooting! Christmas Eve in the dimly-lighted (there was a gas-strike on) front parlour, where the flickering fire-light threw strange shadows on the highly coloured wall-paper, while without, in the wild street, the storm raged pitilessly, and the wind, like some unquiet spirit, flew, moaning, across the square, and passed, wailing with a troubled cry, round by the milk-shop.

We had had supper, and were sitting round, talking and smoking.

We had had a very good supper—a very good supper, indeed. Unpleasantness has occurred since, in our family, in connection with this party. Rumours have been put about in our family, concerning the matter generally, but more particularly concerning my own share in it, and remarks have been passed which have not so much surprised me, because I know what our family are, but which have pained me very much. As for my Aunt Maria, I do not know when I shall care to see her again. I should have thought Aunt Maria might have known me better.

But although injustice—gross injustice, as I shall explain later on-has been done to myself, that shall not deter me from doing justice to others; even to those who have made unfeeling insinuations. I will do justice to Aunt Maria's hot veal pasties, and toasted lobsters, followed by her own special make of cheesecakes, warm (there is no sense, to my thinking, in cold cheesecakes; you lose half the flavour), and washed down by Uncle John's own particular old ale, and acknowledge that they were most tasty. I did justice to them then; Aunt Maria herself could not but admit that.

After supper, Uncle brewed some whisky-punch. I did justice to that also; Uncle John himself said so. He said he was glad to notice that I liked it.

Aunt went to bed soon after supper, leaving the local curate, old Dr. Scrubbles, Mr. Samuel Coombes, our member of the County Council, Teddy Biffles, and myself to keep Uncle company.

We agreed that it was too early to give in for some time yet, so Uncle brewed another bowl of punch; and I think we all did justice to that—at least I know I did. It is a passion with me, is the desire to do justice.

We sat up for a long while, and the Doctor brewed some gin-punch later on, for a change, though I could not taste much difference myself. But it was all good, and we were very happy—everybody was so kind.

Uncle John told us a very funny story in the course of the evening.

Oh, it *was* a funny story! I forget what it was about now, but I know it amused me very much at the time; I do not think I ever laughed so much in all my life. It is strange that I cannot recollect that story too, because he told it us four times. And it was entirely our own fault that he did not tell it us a fifth. After that, the Doctor sang a very clever song, in the course of which he imitated all the different animals in a farmyard. He did mix them a bit. He brayed for the bantam cock, and crowed for the pig; but we knew what he meant all right.

I started relating a most interesting anecdote, but was somewhat surprised to observe, as I went on, that nobody was paying the slightest attention to me whatever. I thought this rather rude of them at first, until it dawned upon me that I was talking to myself all the time, instead of out aloud, so that, of course, they did not know that I was telling them a tale at all, and were probably puzzled to understand the meaning of my animated expression and eloquent gestures. It was a most curious mistake for any one to make. I never knew such a thing happen to me before.

Later on, our curate did tricks with cards. He asked us if we had ever seen a game called the "Three Card Trick." He said it was an artifice by means of which low, unscrupulous men, frequenters of race-meetings and such like haunts, swindled foolish young fellows out of their money. He said it was a very simple trick to do: it all depended on the quickness of the hand. It was the quickness of the hand deceived the eye.

He said he would show us the imposture so that we might be warned against it, and not be taken in by it; and he fetched Uncle's pack of cards from the tea-caddy, and, selecting three cards from the pack, two plain cards and one picture card, sat down on the hearthrug, and explained to us what he was going to do.

He said: "Now I shall take these three cards in my hand—so—and let you all see them. And then I shall quietly lay them down on the rug, with the backs uppermost, and ask you to pick out the picture card. And you'll think you know which one it is." And he did it. Old Mr. Coombes, who is also one of our churchwardens, said it was the middle card.

"You fancy you saw it," said our curate, smiling.

"I don't 'fancy' anything at all about it," replied Mr. Coombes, "I tell you it's the middle card. I'll bet you half a dollar it's the middle card."

"There you are, that's just what I was explaining to you," said our curate, turning to the rest of us; "that's the way these foolish young fellows that I was speaking of are lured on to lose their money. They make sure they know the card, they fancy they saw it. They don't grasp the idea that it is the quickness of the hand that has deceived their eye."

He said he had known young men go off to a boat race, or a cricket match, with pounds in their pocket, and come home, early in the afternoon, stone broke; having lost all their money at this demoralising game.

He said he should take Mr. Coombes's half-crown, because it would teach Mr. Coombes a very useful lesson, and probably be the means of saving Mr. Coombes's money in the future; and he should give the two-and-sixpence to the blanket fund.

"Don't you worry about that," retorted old Mr. Coombes. "Don't you take the half-crown *out* of the blanket fund: that's all."

And he put his money on the middle card, and turned it up.

Sure enough, it really was the queen!

We were all very much surprised, especially the curate. He said that it did sometimes happen that way, though—that a man did sometimes lay on the right card, by accident.

Our curate said it was, however, the most unfortunate thing a man could do for himself, if he only knew it, because, when a man tried and won, it gave him a taste for the so-called sport, and it lured him on into risking again and again; until he had to retire from the contest, a broken and ruined man.

Then he did the trick again. Mr. Coombes said it was the card next the coal-scuttle this time, and wanted to put five shillings on it.

We laughed at him, and tried to persuade him against it. He would listen to no advice, however, but insisted on plunging.

Our curate said very well then: he had warned him, and that was all that he could do. If he (Mr. Coombes) was determined to make a fool of himself, he (Mr. Coombes) must do so.

Our curate said he should take the five shillings and that would put things right again with the blanket fund.

So Mr. Coombes put two half-crowns on the card next the coal-scuttle and turned it up.

Sure enough, it was the queen again!

After that, Uncle John had a florin on, and *he* won.

And then we all played at it; and we all won. All except the curate, that is. He had a very bad quarter of an hour. I never knew a man have such hard luck at cards. He lost every time.

We had some more punch after that; and Uncle made such a funny mistake in brewing it: he left out the whisky. Oh, we did laugh at him, and we made him put in double quantity afterwards, as a forfeit.

Oh, we did have such fun that evening!

And then, somehow or other, we must have got on to ghosts; because the next recollection I have is that we were telling ghost stories to each other.

TEDDY BIFFLES' STORY

Teddy Biffles told the first story, I will let him repeat it here in his own words.

(Do not ask me how it is that I recollect his own exact words—whether I took them down in shorthand at the time, or whether he had the story written out, and handed me the manuscript afterwards for publication in this book, because I should not tell you if you did. It is a trade secret.)

Biffles called his story *Johnson and Emily or The Faithful Ghost.*

JOHNSON AND EMILY
OR
THE FAITHFUL GHOST
(*Teddy Biffles' Story*)

I WAS LITTLE MORE THAN A LAD WHEN I FIRST MET WITH JOHNSON. I was home for the Christmas holidays, and, it being Christmas Eve, I had been allowed to sit up very late. On opening the door of my little bedroom, to go in, I found myself face to face with Johnson, who was coming out. It passed through me, and uttering a long low wail of misery, disappeared out of the staircase window.

I was startled for the moment—I was only a schoolboy at the time, and had never seen a ghost before—and felt a little nervous about going to bed. But, on reflection, I remembered that it was only sinful people that spirits could do any harm to, and so tucked myself up, and went to sleep.

In the morning I told the Pater what I had seen.

"Oh yes, that was old Johnson," he answered. "Don't you be frightened of that; he lives here." And then he told me the poor thing's history.

It seemed that Johnson, when it was alive, had loved, in early life, the daughter of a former lessee of our house, a very beautiful girl, whose Christian name had been Emily. Father did not know her other name.

Johnson was too poor to marry the girl, so he kissed her good-bye, told her he would soon be back, and went off to Australia to make his fortune.

But Australia was not then what it became later on. Travellers through the bush were few and far between in those early days; and, even when one was caught, the portable property found upon the body was often of hardly sufficiently negotiable value to pay the simple

funeral expenses rendered necessary. So that it took Johnson nearly twenty years to make his fortune.

The self-imposed task was accomplished at last, however, and then, having successfully eluded the police, and got clear out of the Colony, he returned to England, full of hope and joy, to claim his bride.

He reached the house to find it silent and deserted. All that the neighbours could tell him was that, soon after his own departure, the family had, on one foggy night, unostentatiously disappeared, and that nobody had ever seen or heard anything of them since, although the landlord and most of the local tradesmen had made searching inquiries.

Poor Johnson, frenzied with grief, sought his lost love all over the world. But he never found her, and, after years of fruitless effort, he returned to end his lonely life in the very house where, in the happy bygone days, he and his beloved Emily had passed so many blissful hours.

He had lived there quite alone, wandering about the empty rooms, weeping and calling to his Emily to come back to him; and when the poor old fellow died, his ghost still kept the business on.

It was there, the Pater said, when he took the house, and the agent had knocked ten pounds a year off the rent in consequence.

After that, I was continually meeting Johnson about the place at all times of the night, and so, indeed, were we all. We used to walk round it and stand aside to let it pass, at first; but, when we grew at home with it, and there seemed no necessity for so much ceremony, we used to walk straight through it. You could not say it was ever much in the way.

It was a gentle, harmless, old ghost, too, and we all felt very sorry for it, and pitied it. The women folk, indeed, made quite a pet of it, for a while. Its faithfulness touched them so.

But as time went on, it grew to be a bit a bore. You see it was full of sadness. There was nothing cheerful or genial about it. You felt sorry for it, but it irritated you. It would sit on the stairs and cry for hours at a stretch; and, whenever we woke up in the night, one was sure to hear it pottering about the passages and in and out of the different rooms, moaning and sighing, so that we could not get to sleep again very easily. And when we had a party on, it would come and sit outside the drawing-room door, and sob all the time. It did not do anybody any harm exactly, but it cast a gloom over the whole affair.

"Oh, I'm getting sick of this old fool," said the Pater, one evening (the Dad can be very blunt, when he is put out, as you know), after Johnson had been more of a nuisance than usual, and had spoiled a good game of whist, by sitting up the chimney and groaning, till nobody knew what were trumps or what suit had been led, even. "We shall have to get rid of him, somehow or other. I wish I knew how to do it."

"Well," said the Mater, "depend upon it, you'll never see the last of him until he's found Emily's grave. That's what he is after. You find Emily's grave, and put him on to that, and he'll stop there. That's the only thing to do. You mark my words."

The idea seemed reasonable, but the difficulty in the way was that we none of us knew where Emily's grave was any more than the ghost of Johnson himself did. The Governor suggested palming off some other Emily's grave upon the poor thing, but, as luck would have it, there did not seem to have been an Emily of any sort buried anywhere for miles round. I never came across a neighbourhood so utterly destitute of dead Emilies.

I thought for a bit, and then I hazarded a suggestion myself.

"Couldn't we fake up something for the old chap?" I queried. "He seems a simple-minded old sort. He might take it in. Anyhow, we could but try."

"By Jove, so we will," exclaimed my father; and the very next morning we had the workmen in, and fixed up a little mound at the bottom of the orchard with a tombstone over it, bearing the following inscription:

Sacred To The Memory Of Emily
Her Last Words Were -
"Tell Johnson I Love Him".

"That ought to fetch him," mused the Dad as he surveyed the work when finished. "I am sure I hope it does."

It did!

We lured him down there that very night; and—well, there, it was one of the most pathetic things I have ever seen, the way Johnson sprang upon that tombstone and wept. Dad and old Squibbins, the gardener, cried like children when they saw it.

Johnson has never troubled us any more in the house since then. It spends every night now, sobbing on the grave, and seems quite happy.

"There still?" Oh yes. I'll take you fellows down and show you it, next time you come to our place: 10 p.m. to 4 a.m. are its general hours, 10 to 2 on Saturdays.

INTERLUDE—THE DOCTOR'S STORY

It made me cry very much, that story, young Biffles told it with so much feeling. We were all a little thoughtful after it, and I noticed even the old Doctor covertly wipe away a tear. Uncle John brewed another bowl of punch, however, and we gradually grew more resigned.

The Doctor, indeed, after a while became almost cheerful, and told us about the ghost of one of his patients.

I cannot give you his story. I wish I could. They all said afterwards that it was the best of the lot—the most ghastly and terrible—but I could not make any sense of it myself. It seemed so incomplete.

He began all right and then something seemed to happen, and then he was finishing it. I cannot make out what he did with the middle of the story.

It ended up, I know, however, with somebody finding something; and that put Mr. Coombes in mind of a very curious affair that took place at an old Mill, once kept by his brother-in-law.

Mr. Coombes said he would tell us his story, and before anybody could stop him, he had begun.

Mr Coombes said the story was called *The Haunted Mill or The Ruined Home.*

THE HAUNTED MILL
OR
THE RUINED HOME
(Mr. Coombes's Story)

WELL, YOU ALL KNOW my brother-in-law, Mr. Parkins (began Mr. Coombes, taking the long clay pipe from his mouth, and putting it behind his ear: we did not know his brother-in-law, but we said we did, so as to save time), and you know of course that he once took a lease of an old Mill in Surrey, and went to live there.

Now you must know that, years ago, this very mill had been occupied by a wicked old miser, who died there, leaving—so it was rumoured—all his money hidden somewhere about the place. Naturally enough, every one who had since come to live at the mill had tried to find the treasure; but none had ever succeeded, and the local wiseacres said that nobody ever would, unless the ghost of the miserly miller should, one day, take a fancy to one of the tenants, and disclose to him the secret of the hiding-place.

My brother-in-law did not attach much importance to the story, regarding it as an old woman's tale, and, unlike his predecessors, made no attempt whatever to discover the hidden gold.

"Unless business was very different then from what it is now," said my brother-in-law, "I don't see how a miller could very well have saved anything, however much of a miser he might have been: at all events, not enough to make it worth the trouble of looking for it."

Still, he could not altogether get rid of the idea of that treasure.

One night he went to bed. There was nothing very extraordinary about that, I admit. He often did go to bed of a night. What *was* remarkable, however, was that exactly as the clock of the village church chimed the last stroke of twelve, my brother-in-law woke up with a start, and felt himself quite unable to go to sleep again.

Joe (his Christian name was Joe) sat up in bed, and looked around. At the foot of the bed something stood very still, wrapped in shadow. It moved into the moonlight, and then my brother-in-law saw that it was the figure of a wizened little old man, in knee-breeches and a pig-tail.

In an instant the story of the hidden treasure and the old miser flashed across his mind.

"He's come to show me where it's hid," thought my brother-in-law; and he resolved that he would not spend all this money on himself, but would devote a small percentage of it towards doing good to others.

The apparition moved towards the door: my brother-in-law put on his trousers and followed it. The ghost went downstairs into the kitchen, glided over and stood in front of the hearth, sighed and disappeared.

Next morning, Joe had a couple of bricklayers in, and made them haul out the stove and pull down the chimney, while he stood behind with a potato-sack in which to put the gold. They knocked down half the wall, and never found so much as a four-penny bit. My brother-in-law did not know what to think.

The next night the old man appeared again, and again led the way into the kitchen. This time, however, instead of going to the fireplace, it stood more in the middle of the room, and sighed there.

"Oh, I see what he means now," said my brother-in-law to himself; "it's under the floor. Why did the old idiot go and stand up against the stove, so as to make me think it was up the chimney?"

They spent the next day in taking up the kitchen floor; but the only thing they found was a three-pronged fork, and the handle of that was broken.

On the third night, the ghost reappeared, quite unabashed, and for a third time made for the kitchen. Arrived there, it looked up at the ceiling and vanished.

"Umph! he don't seem to have learned much sense where he's been to," muttered Joe, as he trotted back to bed; "I should have thought he might have done that at first."

Still, there seemed no doubt now where the treasure lay, and the first thing after breakfast they started pulling down the ceiling. They got every inch of the ceiling down, and they took up the boards of the room above. They discovered about as much treasure as you would expect to find in an empty quart-pot.

On the fourth night, when the ghost appeared, as usual, my brother-in-law was so wild that he threw his boots at it; and the boots passed through the body, and broke a looking-glass.

On the fifth night, when Joe awoke, as he always did now at twelve, the ghost was standing in a dejected attitude, looking very miserable. There was an appealing look in its large sad eyes that quite touched my brother-in-law.

"After all," he thought, "perhaps the silly chap's doing his best. Maybe he has forgotten where he really did put it, and is trying to remember. I'll give him another chance."

The ghost appeared grateful and delighted at seeing Joe prepare to follow him, and led the way into the attic, pointed to the ceiling, and vanished.

"Well, he's hit it this time, I do hope," said my brother-in-law; and next day they set to work to take the roof off the place.

It took them three days to get the roof thoroughly off, and all they found was a bird's nest; after securing which they covered up the house with tarpaulins, to keep it dry.

You might have thought that would have cured the poor fellow of looking for treasure. But it didn't.

He said there must be something in it all, or the ghost would never keep on coming as it did; and that, having gone so far, he would go on to the end, and solve the mystery, cost what it might.

Night after night, he would get out of his bed and follow that spectral old fraud about the house. Each night, the old man would indicate a different place; and, on each following day, my brother-in-law would proceed to break up the mill at the point indicated, and look for the treasure. At the end of three weeks, there was not a room in the mill fit to live in. Every wall had been pulled down, every floor had been taken up, every ceiling had had a hole knocked in it. And then, as suddenly as they had begun, the ghost's visits ceased; and my brother-in-law was left in peace, to rebuild the place at his leisure.

"What induced the old image to play such a silly trick upon a family man and a ratepayer?" Ah! that's just what I cannot tell you.

Some said that the ghost of the wicked old man had done it to punish my brother-in-law for not believing in him at first; while others held that the apparition was probably that of some deceased local plumber and glazier, who would naturally take an interest in seeing a house knocked about and spoilt.

But nobody knew anything for certain.

INTERLUDE

We had some more punch, and then the curate told us a story. I could not make head or tail of the curate's story, so I cannot retail it to you. We none of us could make head or tail of that story. It was a good story enough, so far as material went. There seemed to be an enormous amount of plot, and enough incident to have made a dozen novels. I never before heard a story containing so much incident, nor one dealing with so many varied characters.

I should say that every human being our curate had ever known or met, or heard of, was brought into that story. There were simply hundreds of them. Every five seconds he would introduce into the tale a completely fresh collection of characters accompanied by a brand new set of incidents.

This was the sort of story it was:-

"Well, then, my uncle went into the garden, and got his gun, but, of course, it wasn't there, and Scroggins said he didn't believe it."

"Didn't believe what? Who's Scroggins?"

"Scroggins! Oh, why he was the other man, you know—it was wife."

"*What* was his wife—what's *she* got to do with it?"

"Why, that's what I'm telling you. It was she that found the hat.

She'd come up with her cousin to London—her cousin was my sister-in-law, and the other niece had married a man named Evans, and Evans, after it was all over, had taken the box round to Mr. Jacobs', because Jacobs' father had seen the man, when he was alive, and when he was dead, Joseph—"

"Now look here, never you mind Evans and the box; what's become of your uncle and the gun?"

"The gun! What gun?"

"Why, the gun that your uncle used to keep in the garden, and that wasn't there. What did he do with it? Did he kill any of these people with it—these Jacobses and Evanses and Scrogginses and Josephses? Because, if so, it was a good and useful work, and we should enjoy hearing about it."

"No—oh no—how could he?—he had been built up alive in the wall, you know, and when Edward IV spoke to the abbot about it, my sister said that in her then state of health she could not and would not, as it was endangering the child's life. So they christened it Horatio, after her own son, who had been killed at Waterloo before he was born, and Lord Napier himself said—"

"Look here, do you know what you are talking about?" we asked him at this point.

He said "No," but he knew it was every word of it true, because his aunt had seen it herself. Whereupon we covered him over with the tablecloth, and he went to sleep.

And then Uncle told us a story.

Uncle said his was a real story.

THE GHOST OF THE BLUE CHAMBER

(My Uncle's Story)

"I DON'T WANT to make you fellows nervous," began my uncle in a peculiarly impressive, not to say blood-curdling, tone of voice, "and if you would rather that I did not mention it, I won't; but, as a matter of fact, this very house, in which we are now sitting, is haunted."

"You don't say that!" exclaimed Mr. Coombes.

"What's the use of your saying I don't say it when I have just said it?" retorted my uncle somewhat pettishly. "You do talk so foolishly. I tell you the house is haunted. Regularly on Christmas Eve the Blue Chamber [they called the room next to the nursery the 'blue chamber,' at my uncle's, most of the toilet service being of that shade] is haunted by the ghost of a sinful man—a man who once killed a Christmas wait with a lump of coal."

"How did he do it?" asked Mr. Coombes, with eager anxiousness. "Was it difficult?"

"I do not know how he did it," replied my uncle; "he did not explain the process. The wait had taken up a position just inside the front gate, and was singing a ballad. It is presumed that, when he opened his mouth for B flat, the lump of coal was thrown by the sinful man from one of the windows, and that it went down the wait's throat and choked him."

"You want to be a good shot, but it is certainly worth trying," murmured Mr. Coombes thoughtfully.

"But that was not his only crime, alas!" added my uncle. "Prior to that he had killed a solo cornet-player."

"No! Is that really a fact?" exclaimed Mr. Coombes.

"Of course it's a fact," answered my uncle testily; "at all events, as much a fact as you can expect to get in a case of this sort.

"How very captious you are this evening. The circumstantial evidence was overwhelming. The poor fellow, the cornet-player, had been in the neighbourhood barely a month. Old Mr. Bishop, who kept the 'Jolly Sand Boys' at the time, and from whom I had the story, said he had never known a more hard-working and energetic solo cornet-player. He, the cornet-player, only knew two tunes, but Mr. Bishop said that the man could not have played with more vigour, or for more hours in a day, if he had known forty. The two tunes he did play were "Annie Laurie" and "Home, Sweet Home"; and as regarded his performance of the former melody, Mr. Bishop said that a mere child could have told what it was meant for.

"This musician—this poor, friendless artist used to come regularly and play in this street just opposite for two hours every evening.

One evening he was seen, evidently in response to an invitation, going into this very house, *but was never seen coming out of it!*"

"Did the townsfolk try offering any reward for his recovery?" asked Mr. Coombes.

"Not a ha'penny," replied my uncle.

"Another summer," continued my uncle, "a German band visited here, intending—so they announced on their arrival—to stay till the autumn.

"On the second day from their arrival, the whole company, as fine and healthy a body of men as one could wish to see, were invited to dinner by this sinful man, and, after spending the whole of the next twenty-four hours in bed, left the town a broken and dyspeptic crew; the parish doctor, who had attended them, giving it as his opinion that it was doubtful if they would, any of them, be fit to play an air again."

"You—you don't know the recipe, do you?" asked Mr. Coombes.

"Unfortunately I do not," replied my uncle; "but the chief ingredient was said to have been railway refreshment-room pork-pie.

"I forget the man's other crimes," my uncle went on; "I used to know them all at one time, but my memory is not what it was. I do not, however, believe I am doing his memory an injustice in believing that he was not entirely unconnected with the death, and subsequent burial, of a gentleman who used to play the harp with his toes; and that neither was he altogether unresponsible for the lonely grave of an unknown stranger who had once visited the neighbourhood, an Italian peasant lad, a performer upon the barrel-organ.

"Every Christmas Eve," said my uncle, cleaving with low impressive tones the strange awed silence that, like a shadow, seemed to have slowly stolen into and settled down upon the room, "the ghost of this sinful man haunts the Blue Chamber, in this very house.

There, from midnight until cock-crow, amid wild muffled shrieks and groans and mocking laughter and the ghostly sound of horrid blows, it does fierce phantom fight with the spirits of the solo cornet-player and the murdered wait, assisted at intervals, by the shades of the German band; while the ghost of the strangled harpist plays mad ghostly melodies with ghostly toes on the ghost of a broken harp.

Uncle said the Blue Chamber was comparatively useless as a sleeping-apartment on Christmas Eve.

"Hark!" said uncle, raising a warning hand towards the ceiling, while we held our breath, and listened; "Hark! I believe they are at it now—in the *Blue Chamber!*"

THE BLUE CHAMBER

I rose up, and said that I would sleep in the Blue Chamber. Before I tell you my own story, however—the story of what happened in the Blue Chamber—I would wish to preface it with -

A PERSONAL EXPLANATION

I FEEL A GOOD DEAL OF HESITATION about telling you this story of my own. You see it is not a story like the other stories that I have been telling you, or rather that Teddy Biffles, Mr. Coombes, and my uncle have been telling you: it is a true story. It is not a story told by a person sitting round a fire on Christmas Eve, drinking whisky punch: it is a record of events that actually happened.

Indeed, it is not a 'story' at all, in the commonly accepted meaning of the word: it is a report. It is, I feel, almost out of place in a book of this kind. It is more suitable to a biography, or an English history.

There is another thing that makes it difficult for me to tell you this story, and that is, that it is all about myself. In telling you this story, I shall have to keep on talking about myself; and talking about ourselves is what we modern-day authors have a strong objection to doing. If we literary men of the new school have one praiseworthy yearning more ever present to our minds than another it is the yearning never to appear in the slightest degree egotistical.

I myself, so I am told, carry this coyness—this shrinking reticence concerning anything connected with my own personality, almost too far; and people grumble at me because of it. People come to me and say -

"Well, now, why don't you talk about yourself a bit? That's what we want to read about. Tell us something about yourself."

But I have always replied, "No." It is not that I do not think the subject an interesting one. I cannot myself conceive of any topic more likely to prove fascinating to the world as a whole, or at all events to the cultured portion of it. But I will not do it, on principle. It is inartistic, and it sets a bad example to the younger men. Other writers (a few of them) do it, I know; but I will not—not as a rule.

Under ordinary circumstances, therefore, I should not tell you this story at all. I should say to myself, "No! It is a good story, it is a moral story, it is a strange, weird, enthralling sort of a story; and the public, I know, would like to hear it; and I should like to tell it to them; but it is all about myself—about what I said, and what I saw, and what I did, and I cannot do it. My retiring, anti-egotistical nature will not permit me to talk in this way about myself."

But the circumstances surrounding this story are not ordinary, and there are reasons prompting me, in spite of my modesty, to rather welcome the opportunity of relating it.

As I stated at the beginning, there has been unpleasantness in our family over this party of ours, and, as regards myself in particular, and my share in the events I am now about to set forth, gross injustice has been done me.

As a means of replacing my character in its proper light—of dispelling the clouds of calumny and misconception with which it has been darkened, I feel that my best course is to give a simple, dignified narration of the plain facts, and allow the unprejudiced to judge for themselves. My chief object, I candidly confess, is to clear myself from unjust aspersion. Spurred by this motive—and I think it is an honourable and a right motive—I find I am enabled to overcome my usual repugnance to talking about myself, and can thus tell—

MY OWN STORY

As soon as my uncle had finished his story, I, as I have already told you, rose up and said that I would sleep in the Blue Chamber that very night.

"Never!" cried my uncle, springing up. "You shall not put yourself in this deadly peril. Besides, the bed is not made."

"Never mind the bed," I replied. "I have lived in furnished apartments for gentlemen, and have been accustomed to sleep on beds that have never been made from one year's end to the other. Do not thwart me in my resolve. I am young, and have had a clear conscience now for over a month. The spirits will not harm me. I may even do them some little good, and induce them to be quiet and go away. Besides, I should like to see the show."

Saying which, I sat down again. (How Mr. Coombes came to be in my chair, instead of at the other side of the room, where he had been all the evening; and why he never offered to apologise when I sat right down on top of him; and why young Biffles should have tried to palm himself off upon me as my Uncle John, and induced me, under that erroneous impression, to shake him by the hand for nearly three minutes, and tell him that I had always regarded him as father,—are matters that, to this day, I have never been able to fully understand.)

They tried to dissuade me from what they termed my foolhardy enterprise, but I remained firm, and claimed my privilege. I was 'the guest.' 'The guest' always sleeps in the haunted chamber on Christmas Eve; it is his perquisite.

They said that if I put it on that footing, they had, of course, no answer; and they lighted a candle for me, and accompanied me upstairs in a body.

Whether elevated by the feeling that I was doing a noble action, or animated by a mere general consciousness of rectitude, is not for me to say, but I went upstairs that night with remarkable buoyancy. It was as much as I could do to stop at the landing when I came to it; I felt I wanted to go on up to the roof. But, with the help of the banisters, I restrained my ambition, wished them all good-night, and went in and shut the door.

Things began to go wrong with me from the very first. The candle tumbled out of the candlestick before my hand was off the lock. It kept on tumbling out of the candlestick, and every time I picked put it up and put it in, it tumbled out again: I never saw such a slippery candle. I gave up attempting to use the candlestick at last, and carried the candle about in my hand; and, even then, it would not keep upright. So I got wild and threw it out of window, and undressed and went to bed in the dark.

I did not go to sleep—I did not feel sleepy at all—I lay on my back, looking up at the ceiling, and thinking of things. I wish I could remember some of the ideas that came to me as I lay there, because they were so amusing. I laughed at them myself till the bed shook.

I had been lying like this for half an hour or so, and had forgotten all about the ghost, when, on casually casting my eyes round the room, I noticed for the first time a singularly contented-looking phantom, sitting in the easy-chair by the fire, smoking the ghost of a long clay pipe.

I fancied for the moment, as most people would under similar circumstances, that I must be dreaming. I sat up, and rubbed my eyes.

No! It was a ghost, clear enough. I could see the back of the chair through his body. He looked over towards me, took the shadowy pipe from his lips, and nodded.

The most surprising part of the whole thing to me was that I did not feel in the least alarmed. If anything, I was rather pleased to see him. It was company.

I said, "Good evening. It's been a cold day!"

He said he had not noticed it himself, but dared say I was right.

We remained silent for a few seconds, and then, wishing to put it pleasantly, I said, "I believe I have the honour of addressing the ghost of the gentleman who had the accident with the wait?"

He smiled, and said it was very good of me to remember it. One wait was not much to boast of, but still, every little helped.

I was somewhat staggered at his answer. I had expected a groan of remorse. The ghost appeared, on the contrary, to be rather conceited over the business. I thought that, as he had taken my reference to the wait so quietly, perhaps he would not be offended if I questioned him about the organ-grinder. I felt curious about that poor boy.

"Is it true," I asked, "that you had a hand in the death of that Italian peasant lad who came to the town once with a barrel-organ that played nothing but Scotch airs?"

He quite fired up. "Had a hand in it!" he exclaimed indignantly. "Who has dared to pretend that he assisted me? I murdered the youth myself. Nobody helped me. Alone I did it. Show me the man who says I didn't."

I calmed him. I assured him that I had never, in my own mind, doubted that he was the real and only assassin, and I went on and asked him what he had done with the body of the cornet-player he had killed.

He said, "To which one may you be alluding?"

"Oh, were there any more then?" I inquired.

He smiled, and gave a little cough. He said he did not like to appear to be boasting, but that, counting trombones, there were seven.

"Dear me!" I replied, "you must have had quite a busy time of it, one way and another."

He said that perhaps he ought not to be the one to say so, but that really, speaking of ordinary middle-society, he thought there were few ghosts who could look back upon a life of more sustained usefulness.

He puffed away in silence for a few seconds, while I sat watching him. I had never seen a ghost smoking a pipe before, that I could remember, and it interested me.

I asked him what tobacco he used, and he replied, "The ghost of cut cavendish, as a rule."

He explained that the ghost of all the tobacco that a man smoked in life belonged to him when he became dead. He said he himself had smoked a good deal of cut cavendish when he was alive, so that he was well supplied with the ghost of it now.

I observed that it was a useful thing to know that, and I made up my mind to smoke as much tobacco as ever I could before I died.

I thought I might as well start at once, so I said I would join him in a pipe, and he said, "Do, old man"; and I reached over and got out the necessary paraphernalia from my coat pocket and lit up.

We grew quite chummy after that, and he told me all his crimes. He said he had lived next door once to a young lady who was learning to play the guitar, while a gentleman who practised on the bass-viol lived opposite. And he, with fiendish cunning, had introduced these two unsuspecting young people to one another, and had persuaded them to elope with each other against their parents' wishes, and take their musical instruments with them; and they had done so, and, before the honeymoon was over, *she* had broken his head with the bass-viol, and *he* had tried to cram the guitar down her throat, and had injured her for life.

My friend said he used to lure muffin-men into the passage and then stuff them with their own wares till they burst and died. He said he had quieted eighteen that way.

Young men and women who recited long and dreary poems at evening parties, and callow youths who walked about the streets late at night, playing concertinas, he used to get together and poison in batches of ten, so as to save expense; and park orators and temperance lecturers he used to shut up six in a small room with a glass of water and a collection-box apiece, and let them talk each other to death.

It did one good to listen to him.

I asked him when he expected the other ghosts—the ghosts of the wait and the cornet-player, and the German band that Uncle John had mentioned. He smiled, and said they would never come again, any of them.

I said, "Why; isn't it true, then, that they meet you here every Christmas Eve for a row?"

He replied that it *was* true. Every Christmas Eve, for twenty-five years, had he and they fought in that room; but they would never trouble him nor anybody else again. One by one, had he laid them out, spoilt, and utterly useless for all haunting purposes. He had finished off the last German-band ghost that very evening, just before I came upstairs, and had thrown what was left of it out through the slit between the window-sashes. He said it would never be worth calling a ghost again.

"I suppose you will still come yourself, as usual?" I said. "They would be sorry to miss you, I know."

"Oh, I don't know," he replied; "there's nothing much to come for now. Unless," he added kindly, "*you* are going to be here. I'll come if you will sleep here next Christmas Eve."

"I have taken a liking to you," he continued; "you don't fly off, screeching, when you see a party, and your hair doesn't stand on end. You've no idea," he said, "how sick I am of seeing people's hair standing on end."

He said it irritated him.

Just then a slight noise reached us from the yard below, and he started and turned deathly black.

"You are ill," I cried, springing towards him; "tell me the best thing to do for you. Shall I drink some brandy, and give you the ghost of it?"

He remained silent, listening intently for a moment, and then he gave a sigh of relief, and the shade came back to his cheek.

"It's all right," he murmured; "I was afraid it was the cock."

"Oh, it's too early for that," I said. "Why, it's only the middle of the night."

"Oh, that doesn't make any difference to those cursed chickens," he replied bitterly. "They would just as soon crow in the middle of the night as at any other time—sooner, if they thought it would spoil a chap's evening out. I believe they do it on purpose."

He said a friend of his, the ghost of a man who had killed a water-rate collector, used to haunt a house in Long Acre, where they kept fowls in the cellar, and every time a policeman went by and flashed his bull's-eye down the grating, the old cock there would fancy it was the sun, and start crowing like mad; when, of course, the poor ghost had to dissolve, and it would, in consequence, get back home sometimes as early as one o'clock in the morning, swearing fearfully because it had only been out for an hour.

I agreed that it seemed very unfair.

"Oh, it's an absurd arrangement altogether," he continued, quite angrily. "I can't imagine what our old man could have been thinking of when he made it. As I have said to him, over and over again, 'Have a fixed time, and let everybody stick to it—say four o'clock in summer, and six in winter. Then one would know what one was about.'"

"How do you manage when there isn't any cock handy?" I inquired.

He was on the point of replying, when again he started and listened. This time I distinctly heard Mr. Bowles's cock, next door, crow twice.

"There you are," he said, rising and reaching for his hat; "that's the sort of thing we have to put up with. What *is* the time?"

I looked at my watch, and found it was half-past three.

"I thought as much," he muttered. "I'll wring that blessed bird's neck if I get hold of it." And he prepared to go.

"If you can wait half a minute," I said, getting out of bed, "I'll go a bit of the way with you."

"It's very good of you," he rejoined, pausing, "but it seems unkind to drag you out."

"Not at all," I replied; "I shall like a walk." And I partially dressed myself, and took my umbrella; and he put his arm through mine, and we went out together.

Just by the gate we met Jones, one of the local constables.

"Good-night, Jones," I said (I always feel affable at Christmas-time).

"Good-night, sir," answered the man a little gruffly, I thought. "May I ask what you're a-doing of?"

"Oh, it's all right," I responded, with a wave of my umbrella; "I'm just seeing my friend part of the way home."

He said, "What friend?"

"Oh, ah, of course," I laughed; "I forgot. He's invisible to you. He is the ghost of the gentleman that killed the wait. I'm just going to the corner with him."

"Ah, I don't think I would, if I was you, sir," said Jones severely. "If you take my advice, you'll say good-bye to your friend here, and go back indoors. Perhaps you are not aware that you are walking about with nothing on but a night-shirt and a pair of boots and an opera-hat. Where's your trousers?"

I did not like the man's manner at all. I said, "Jones! I don't wish to have to report you, but it seems to me you've been drinking. My trousers are where a man's trousers ought to be—on his legs. I distinctly remember putting them on."

"Well, you haven't got them on now," he retorted.

"I beg your pardon," I replied. "I tell you I have; I think I ought to know."

"I think so, too," he answered, "but you evidently don't. Now you come along indoors with me, and don't let's have any more of it."

Uncle John came to the door at this point, having been awaked, I suppose, by the altercation; and, at the same moment, Aunt Maria appeared at the window in her nightcap.

I explained the constable's mistake to them, treating the matter as lightly as I could, so as not to get the man into trouble, and I turned for confirmation to the ghost.

He was gone! He had left me without a word—without even saying good-bye!

It struck me as so unkind, his having gone off in that way, that I burst into tears; and Uncle John came out, and led me back into the house.

On reaching my room, I discovered that Jones was right. I had not put on my trousers, after all. They were still hanging over the bed-rail. I suppose, in my anxiety not to keep the ghost waiting, I must have forgotten them.

Such are the plain facts of the case, out of which it must, doubtless, to the healthy, charitable mind appear impossible that calumny could spring.

But it has.

Persons—I say 'persons'—have professed themselves unable to understand the simple circumstances herein narrated, except in the light of explanations at once misleading and insulting. Slurs have been cast and aspersions made on me by those of my own flesh and blood.

But I bear no ill-feeling. I merely, as I have said, set forth this statement for the purpose of clearing my character from injurious suspicion.

Clocks

From a volume entitled "*Diary of a Pilgrimage*"

By Jerome K. Jerome

There are two kinds of clocks. There is the clock that is always wrong, and that knows it is wrong, and glories in it; and there is the clock that is always right—except when you rely upon it, and then it is more wrong than you would think a clock *could* be in a civilized country.

I remember a clock of this latter type, that we had in the house when I was a boy, routing us all up at three o'clock one winter's morning. We had finished breakfast at ten minutes to four, and I got to school a little after five, and sat down on the step outside and cried, because I thought the world had come to an end; everything was so death-like!

The man who can live in the same house with one of these clocks, and not endanger his chance of heaven about once a month by standing up and telling it what he thinks of it, is either a dangerous rival to that old established firm, Job, or else he does not know enough bad language to make it worth his while to start saying anything at all.

The great dream of its life is to lure you on into trying to catch a train by it. For weeks and weeks it will keep the most perfect time. If there were any difference in time between that clock and the sun, you would be convinced it was the sun, not the clock, that wanted seeing to.

You feel that if that clock happened to get a quarter of a second fast, or the eighth of an instant slow, it would break its heart and die. It is in this spirit of child-like faith in its integrity that, one morning, you gather your family around you in the passage, kiss your children, thoroughly depend upon; but you wanted to know it—to have studied its system. An outsider might be easily misled by it.

"For instance," he would say, "when it strikes fifteen, and the hands point to twenty minutes past eleven, I know it is a quarter to eight."

His acquaintanceship with that clock must certainly have given him an advantage over the cursory observer!

But the great charm about my clock is its reliable uncertainty. It works on no method whatever; it is a pure emotionalist. One day it will be quite frolicsome, and gain three hours in the course of the morning, and think nothing of it; and the next day it will wish it were dead, and be hardly able to drag itself along, and lose two hours out of every four, and stop altogether in the afternoon, too miserable to do anything; and then, getting cheerful once more toward evening, will start off again of its own accord.

I do not care to talk much about this clock; because when I tell the simple truth concerning it, people think I am exaggerating.

It is very discouraging to find, when you are straining every nerve to tell the truth, that people do not believe you, and fancy that you are exaggerating. It makes you feel inclined to go and exaggerate on purpose, just to show them the difference. I know I often feel tempted to do so myself—it is my early training that saves me.

We should always be very careful never to give way to exaggeration; it is a habit that grows upon one.

And it is such a vulgar habit, too. In the old times, when poets and dry-goods salesmen were the only people who exaggerated, there was something clever and *distingue* about a reputation for "a tendency to over, rather than to under-estimate the mere bald facts." But everybody exaggerates nowadays. The art of exaggeration is no longer regarded as an "extra" in the modern bill of education; it is an essential requirement, held to be most needful for the battle of life.

The whole world exaggerates. It exaggerates everything, from the yearly number of bicycles sold to the yearly number of heathens converted—into the hope of salvation and more whiskey. Exaggeration is the basis of our trade, the fallow-field of our art and literature, the groundwork of our social life, the foundation of our political existence.

and afterward wipe your jammy mouth, poke your finger in the baby's eye, promise not to forget to order the coals, wave at last fond adieu with the umbrella, and depart for the railway-station.

I never have been quite able to decide, myself, which is the more irritating to run two miles at the top of your speed, and then to find, when you reach the station, that you are three-quarters of an hour too early; or to stroll along leisurely the whole way, and dawdle about outside the booking-office, talking to some local idiot, and then to swagger carelessly on to the platform, just in time to see the train go out!

As for the other class of clocks—the common or always-wrong clocks—they are harmless enough. You wind them up at the proper intervals, and once or twice a week you put them right and "regulate" them, as you call it (and you might just as well try to "regulate" a London tom-cat). But you do all this, not from any selfish motives, but from a sense of duty to the clock itself. You want to feel that, whatever may happen, you have done the right thing by it, and that no blame can attach to you.

So far as looking to it for any return is concerned, that you never dream of doing, and consequently you are not disappointed. You ask what the time is, and the girl replies:

"Well, the clock in the dining-room says a quarter past two."

But you are not deceived by this. You know that, as a matter of fact, it must be somewhere between nine and ten in the evening; and, remembering that you noticed, as a curious circumstance, that the clock was only forty minutes past four, hours ago, you mildly admire its energies and resources, and wonder how it does it.

I myself possess a clock that for complicated unconventionality and light-hearted independence, could, I should think, give points to anything yet discovered in the chronometrical line. As a mere time-piece, it leaves much to be desired; but, considered as a self-acting conundrum, it is full of interest and variety.

I heard of a man once who had a clock that he used to say was of no good to any one except himself, because he was the only man who understood it. He said it was an excellent clock, and one that you could

As schoolboys, we exaggerate our fights and our marks and our fathers' debts. As men, we exaggerate our wares, we exaggerate our feelings, we exaggerate our incomes—except to the tax-collector, and to him we exaggerate our "outgoings"; we exaggerate our virtues; we even exaggerate our vices, and, being in reality the mildest of men, pretend we are dare-devil scamps.

We have sunk so low now that we try to *act* our exaggerations, and to live up to our lies. We call it "keeping up appearances;" and no more bitter phrase could, perhaps, have been invented to describe our childish folly.

If we possess a hundred pounds a year, do we not call it two? Our larder may be low and our grates be chill, but we are happy if the "world" (six acquaintances and a prying neighbor) gives us credit for one hundred and fifty. And, when we have five hundred, we talk of a thousand, and the all-important and beloved "world" (sixteen friends now, and two of them carriage-folks!) agree that we really must be spending seven hundred, or at all events, running into debt up to that figure; but the butcher and baker, who have gone into the matter with the housemaid, know better.

After awhile, having learned the trick, we launch out boldly and spend like Indian Princes—or rather *seem* to spend; for we know, by this time, how to purchase the seeming with the seeming, how to bu

y the appearance of wealth with the appearance of cash. And the dear old world—Beelzebub bless it! for it is his own child, sure enough; there is no mistaking the likeness, it has all his funny little ways—gathers round, applauding and laughing at the lie, and sharing in the cheat, and gloating over the thought of the blow that it knows must sooner or later fall on us from the Thor-like hammer of Truth.

And all goes merry as a witches' frolic—until the gray morning dawns.

Truth and fact are old-fashioned and out-of-date, my friends, fit only for the dull and vulgar to live by. Appearance, not reality, is what the clever dog grasps at in these clever days. We spurn the dull-brown solid earth; we build our lives and homes in the fair-seeming rainbow-land of shadow and chimera.

To ourselves, sleeping and waking there, *behind* the rainbow, there is no beauty in the house; only a chill damp mist in every room, and, over all, a haunting fear of the hour when the gilded clouds will melt away, and let us fall—somewhat heavily, no doubt—upon the hard world underneath.

But, there! of what matter is *our* misery, *our* terror? To the stranger, our home appears fair and bright. The workers in the fields below look up and envy us our abode of glory and delight! If *they* think it pleasant, surely *we* should be content. Have we not been taught to live for others and not for ourselves, and are we not acting up bravely to the teaching—in this most curious method?

Ah! yes, we are self-sacrificing enough, and loyal enough in our devotion to this new-crowned king, the child of Prince Imposture and Princess Pretense. Never before was despot so blindly worshiped! Never had earthly sovereign yet such world-wide sway!

Man, if he would live, *must* worship. He looks around, and what to him, within the vision of his life, is the greatest and the best, that he falls down and does reverence to. To him whose eyes have opened on the nineteenth century, what nobler image can the universe produce than the figure of Falsehood in stolen robes? It is cunning and brazen and hollow-hearted, and it realizes his souls ideal, and he falls and kisses its feet, and clings to its skinny knees, swearing fealty to it for evermore!

Ah! he is a mighty monarch, bladder-bodied King Humbug! Come, let us build up temples of hewn shadows wherein we may adore him, safe from the light. Let us raise him aloft upon our Brummagem shields. Long live our coward, falsehearted chief!—fit leader for such soldiers as we! Long live the Lord of-Lies, anointed! Long live poor King Appearances, to whom all mankind bows the knee!

But we must hold him aloft very carefully, oh, my brother warriors! He needs much "keeping up." He has no bones and sinews of his own, the poor old flimsy fellow! If we take our hands from him, he will fall a heap of worn-out rags, and the angry wind will whirl him away, and leave us forlorn. Oh, let us spend our lives keeping him up, and serving him, and making him great—that is, evermore puffed out with air and nothingness—until he burst, and we along with him!

Burst one day he must, as it is in the nature of bubbles to burst, especially when they grow big. Meanwhile, he still reigns over us, and the world grows more and more a world of pretense and exaggeration and lies; and he who pretends and exaggerates and lies the most successfully, is the greatest of us all.

The world is a gingerbread fair, and we all stand outside our booths and point to the gorgeous-colored pictures, and beat the big drum and brag.

Brag! brag! Life is one great game of brag!

"Buy my soap, oh ye people, and ye will never look old, and the hair will grow again on your bald places, and ye will never be poor or unhappy again; and mine is the only true soap. Oh, beware of spurious imitations!"

"Buy my lotion, all ye that suffer from pains in the head, or the stomach, or the feet, or that have broken arms, or broken hearts, or objectionable mothers-in-law; and drink one bottle a day, and all your troubles will be ended."

"Come to my church, all ye that want to go to Heaven, and buy my penny weekly guide, and pay my pew-rates; and, pray ye, have nothing to do with my misguided brother over the road. *This* is the only safe way!"

"Oh, vote for me, my noble and intelligent electors, and send our party into power, and the world shall be a new place, and there shall be no sin or sorrow any more! And each free and independent voter shall have a bran new Utopia made on purpose for him, according to his own ideas, with a good-sized, extra-unpleasant purgatory attached, to which he can send everybody he does not like. Oh! do not miss this chance!"

Oh! listen to my philosophy, it is the best and deepest. Oh! hear my songs, they are the sweetest. Oh! buy my pictures, they alone are true art. Oh! read my books, they are the finest.

Oh! *I* am the greatest cheesemonger, *I* am the greatest soldier, *I* am the greatest statesman, *I* am the greatest poet, *I* am the greatest showman, *I* am the greatest mountebank, *I* am the greatest editor, and *I* am the greatest patriot. *We* are the greatest nation. *We* are the only good people. *Ours* is the only true religion. Bah! how we all yell!

How we all brag and bounce, and beat the drum and shout; and nobody believes a word we utter; and the people ask one another, saying:

"How can we tell who is the greatest and the cleverest among all these shrieking braggarts?"

And they answer:

"There is none great or clever. The great and clever men are not here; there is no place for them in this pandemonium of charlatans and quacks. The men you see here are crowing cocks. We suppose the greatest and the best of *them* are they who crow the loudest and the longest; that is the only test of *their* merits."

Therefore, what is left for us to do, but to crow? And the best and greatest of us all, is he who crows the loudest and the longest on this little dunghill that we call our world!

Well, I was going to tell you about our clock.

It was my wife's idea, getting it, in the first instance. We had been to dinner at the Buggles', and Buggles had just bought a clock—"picked it up in Essex," was the way he described the transaction. Buggles is always going about "picking up" things. He will stand before an old carved bedstead, weighing about three tons, and say:

"Yes—pretty little thing! I picked it up in Holland;" as though he had found it by the roadside, and slipped it into his umbrella when nobody was looking!

Buggles was rather full of this clock. It was of the good old-fashioned "grandfather" type. It stood eight feet high, in a carved-oak case, and had a deep, sonorous, solemn tick, that made a pleasant accompaniment to the after-dinner chat, and seemed to fill the room with an air of homely dignity.

We discussed the clock, and Buggles said how he loved the sound of its slow, grave tick; and how, when all the house was still, and he and it were sitting up alone together, it seemed like some wise old friend talking to him, and telling him about the old days and the old ways of thought, and the old life and the old people.

The clock impressed my wife very much. She was very thoughtful all the way home, and, as we went upstairs to our flat, she said, "Why could not we have a clock like that?" She said it would seem like having some one in the house to take care of us all—she should fancy it was looking after baby!

I have a man in Northamptonshire from whom I buy old furniture now and then, and to him I applied. He answered by return to say that he had got exactly the very thing I wanted. (He always has. I am very lucky in this respect.) It was the quaintest and most old-fashioned clock he had come across for a long while, and he enclosed photograph and full particulars; should he send it up?

From the photograph and the particulars, it seemed, as he said, the very thing, and I told him, "Yes; send it up at once."

Three days afterward, there came a knock at the door—there had been other knocks at the door before this, of course; but I am dealing merely with the history of the clock. The girl said a couple of men were outside, and wanted to see me, and I went to them.

I found they were Pickford's carriers, and glancing at the way-bill, I saw that it was my clock that they had brought, and I said, airily, "Oh, yes, it's quite right; bring it up!"

They said they were very sorry, but that was just the difficulty. They could not get it up.

I went down with them, and wedged securely across the second landing of the staircase, I found a box which I should have judged to be the original case in which Cleopatra's Needle came over.

They said that was my clock.

I brought down a chopper and a crowbar, and we sent out and collected in two extra hired ruffians and the five of us worked away for half an hour and got the clock out; after which the traffic up and down the staircase was resumed, much to the satisfaction of the other tenants.

We then got the clock upstairs and put it together, and I fixed it in the corner of the dining-room.

At first it exhibited a strong desire to topple over and fall on people, but by the liberal use of nails and screws and bits of firewood, I made life in the same room with it possible, and then, being exhausted, I had my wounds dressed, and went to bed.

In the middle of the night my wife woke me up in a great state of alarm, to say that the clock had just struck thirteen, and who did I think was going to die?

I said I did not know, but hoped it might be the next-door dog.

My wife said she had a presentiment it meant baby. There was no comforting her; she cried herself to sleep again.

During the course of the morning, I succeeded in persuading her that she must have made a mistake, and she consented to smile once more. In the afternoon the clock struck thirteen again.

This renewed all her fears. She was convinced now that both baby and I were doomed, and that she would be left a childless widow. I tried to treat the matter as a joke, and this only made her more wretched.

She said that she could see I really felt as she did, and was only pretending to be light-hearted for her sake, and she said she would try and bear it bravely.

The person she chiefly blamed was Buggles.

In the night the clock gave us another warning, and my wife accepted it for her Aunt Maria, and seemed resigned. She wished, however, that I had never had the clock, and wondered when, if ever, I should get cured of my absurd craze for filling the house with tomfoolery.

The next day the clock struck thirteen four times and this cheered her up. She said that if we were all going to die, it did not so much matter. Most likely there was a fever or a plague coming, and we should all be taken together.

She was quite light-hearted over it!

After that the clock went on and killed every friend and relation we had, and then it started on the neighbors.

It struck thirteen all day long for months, until we were sick of slaughter, and there could not have been a human being left alive for miles around.

Then it turned over a new leaf, and gave up murdering folks, and took to striking mere harmless thirty-nines and forty-ones. Its favorite number now is thirty-two, but once a day it strikes forty-nine. It never strikes more than forty-nine. I don't know why—I have never been able to understand why—but it doesn't.

It does not strike at regular intervals, but when it feels it wants to and would be better for it. Sometimes it strikes three or four times within the same hour, and at other times it will go for half-a-day without striking at all.

He is an odd old fellow!

I have thought now and then of having him "seen to," and made to keep regular hours and be respectable; but, somehow, I seem to have grown to love him as he is with his daring mockery of Time.

He certainly has not much respect for it. He seems to go out of his way almost to openly insult it. He calls half-past two thirty-eight o'clock, and in twenty minutes from then he says it is one!

Is it that he really has grown to feel contempt for his master, and wishes to show it? They say no man is a hero to his valet; may it be that even stony-face Time himself is but a short-lived, puny mortal—a little greater than some others, that is all—to the dim eyes of this old servant of his? Has he, ticking, ticking, all these years, come at last to see into the littleness of that Time that looms so great to our awed human eyes?

Is he saying, as he grimly laughs, and strikes his thirty-fives and forties: "Bah! I know you, Time, godlike and dread though you seem. What are you but a phantom—a dream—like the rest of us here? Ay, less, for you will pass away and be no more. Fear him not, immortal men. Time is but the shadow of the world upon the background of Eternity!"

Jerome Klapka Jerome

Jerome Klapka Jerome (May 2, 1859 – June 14, 1927) was an English writer and humorist, best known for the humorous travelogue *Three Men in a Boat.*

Jerome was born in Caldmore, Walsall, England. Jerome was the fourth child of Jerome Clapp Jerome, minister and part-time farmer, and Marguerite Jones.

Due to bad investments in the local mining industry, the family suffered poverty, and debt collectors often visited, an experience Jerome described vividly in his autobiography *My Life and Times.*

The young Jerome wished to go into politics or be a man of letters, but the death of both his parents in 1872, when he was 13 years old, forced him to quit his studies and find work to support himself. He was employed at the London and North Western Railway, initially collecting coal that fell along the railway, and remained there for four years.

ACTING CAREER AND EARLY LITERARY WORKS

In 1877, inspired by his older sister's love for the theatre, Jerome had decided to try his hand at acting, under the stage name Harold Crichton. He joined a repertory troupe who tried to produce plays on a shoestring budget. Jerome had later comically reflected on this period in *On the Stage — and Off.* After three years on the road Jerome tried to become a journalist, but most of his writings were rejected. Finally, in 1885, he had some success with *On the Stage — and Off* and *Idle Thoughts of an Idle Fellow* followed in 1886. On 21 June

1888, Jerome married Georgina Elizabeth Henrietta Stanley Marris, who would later be known in his works as Ettie.

THREE MAN IN A BOAT AND LATER CAREER

Jerome sat down to write *Three Men in a Boat* as soon as the couple returned from their honeymoon. In the novel, his wife was replaced by his longtime friends George Wingrave (George) and Carl Hentschel (Harris). The book, published in 1889, became an instant success. With the financial security the sales of the book provided, Jerome was able to dedicate all of his time to writing. In 1892 he was chosen by Robert Barr to edit *The Idler* over Rudyard Kipling. In 1893 he founded *To-Day*, but had to withdraw from both publications because of financial difficulties and a libel suit.

In 1898, a short stay in Germany inspired *Three Men on the Bummel.* In 1902 he published the novel *Paul Kelver*, which was widely praised and by some critics considered worthy to be put alongside Dickens. His 1908 play *The Passing of the Third Floor Back* introduced a more sombre and religious Jerome.

WORLD WAR I AND LAST YEARS

Jerome volunteered to serve his country at the outbreak of the war but, being 56 years old, was rejected by the British Army. He then volunteered as an ambulance driver for the French Army. The war experience dampened his spirit, as did the death in 1921 of his stepdaughter, Elsie.

In 1926, Jerome published his autobiography, *My Life and Times.* Shortly afterwards, the Borough of Walsall conferred on him the title Freeman of the Borough. In June 1927, on a motoring tour from Devon to London via Cheltenham and Northampton, Jerome suffered a paralytic stroke and a cerebral haemorrhage. He lay in Northampton General Hospital for two weeks before succumbing on 14 June. He was cremated at Golders Green and his ashes buried at St Mary's Church, Ewelme, Oxfordshire.

THE JEROME K JEROME SOCIETY

(excepts from the society's web site)

The Society was formed in 1984 with the main object of stimulating interest in and public awareness of the life and works of Jerome K. Jerome. The incentive to its formation was the opening, in July 1984, of a small museum in Belsize House, Walsall—the author's birthplace. A major aim is to provide financial support to the museum so that it may stand as a lasting memorial to Jerome in the town of his birth and serve as a focus for all devotees of the man and his works.

The building had languished in a semi-derelict state for many years, when the property eventually came up for sale in 1984. Gordon H. Foster M.B.E. took a great risk and bought it. With the help of a modest grant (it is a listed building) he restored it and created, on the ground floor, two rooms dedicated to the memory of Jerome K. Jerome.

However as a condition to keeping the museum open the Walsall Borough Council requested a Jerome K. Jerome Society to be formed, in order to raise funds on an annual basis. The society was duly formed and, after a slow start, has flourished and has now members from all parts of the globe including America, Madagascar, Canada, Australia and Italy.

Members of the Society, whilst supporting this very good cause also manage to enjoy themselves at every opportunity. They don straw boaters and striped blazers and take to the boats fortified by Champagne and memories of Jerome's intrepid trio (to say nothing of the dog). The annual dinner has become a really sparkling event and has featured many illustrious guest speaker.

As of July 2007 the Museum has been closed due to the withdrawal of the grant (£2,000) by the Walsall Metropolitan Borough Council. Alternative arrangements are being made. For more details visit the Society's website:

http://www.jeromekjerome.com

BIBLIOGRAPHY

NOVELS

Idle Thoughts of an Idle Fellow (1886)
Three Men in a Boat (1889)
Diary of a Pilgrimage (and Six Essays) (1891)
Novel Notes (1893)
Second Thoughts of an Idle Fellow (1898)
Three Men on the Bummel (Three Men on Wheels) (1900)
Paul Kelver, a novel (1902)
Tommy and Co (1904)
They and I (1909)
All Roads Lead to Calvary (1919)
Anthony John (1923)
The Love of Ulrich Nebendahl (1909)
The Philosopher's Joke (1909)

COLLECTIONS

Told After Supper (1891)
John Ingerfield: And Other Stories (1894)
Sketches in Lavender, Blue and Green (1895)
The Observations of Henry (1901)
The Angel and the Author and Others (1904)
American Wives and Others (1904)
The Passing of the Third Floor Back: And Other Stories (1907)
Malvina of Brittany (1916)
A miscellany of sense and nonsense from the writings of Jerome K. Jerome. Selected by the author with many apologies, with forty-three illustrations by Will Owen. 1924

AUTOBIOGRAPHY

My Life and Times (1926)

Short stories

The Haunted Mill (1891)
The New Utopia (1891)
The Dancing Partner (1893)
Christmas Eve in the Blue Chamber
Silhouettes
The Skeleton
The Snake
The Woman of the Saeter

Plays

The Maister of Wood Barrow: play in three acts (1890)
The Night of Feb. 14th. 1899: a play in nine scenes
Miss Hobbs: a comedy in four acts (1902)
Fanny and the Servant Problem, a quite possible play in four acts (1909)
The Master of Mrs. Chilvers: an improbable comedy (1911)
The Celebrity: a play in three acts (1926)
Robina's Web ("The Dovecote" or "The grey feather"): a farce in four acts

www.ingramcontent.com/pod-product-compliance
Ingram Content Group UK Ltd.
Pitfield, Milton Keynes, MK11 3LW, UK
UKHW020231250726
13967UKWH00001B/302

9 781409 229445